PAST YO
DATE YET?

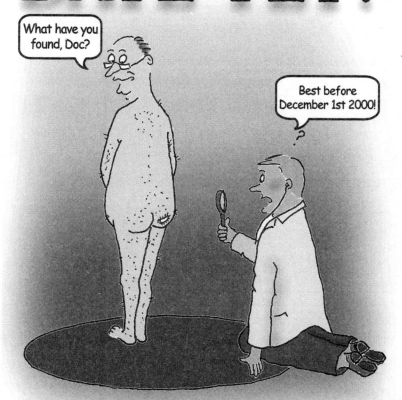

AN AMUSING INSIGHT INTO
THAT PEAK PERIOD IN ONE'S LIFE...

Illustrations by
Bob Gibbs

Crombie Jardine
PUBLISHING LIMITED
Office 2, 3 Edgar Buildings
George Street
Bath
BA1 2FJ
www.crombiejardine.com

Published by Crombie Jardine Publishing Limited
First edition, 2006

ISBN 1-905102-80-1 (10-digit)

ISBN 978-1-905102-80-8 (13-digit)

Illustrations by Bob Gibbs
Designed by www.glensaville.com
Printed and bound in Great Britain by
Cox and Wyman Ltd, Reading, Berks

INTRODUCTION

PAST YOUR SELL-BY DATE YET?

The advances in medical science have resulted in many of us now living way past our sell-by date. Ageing brings us new problems but with a sense of humour and a lifetime of experience we can look getting old in the face and blow a raspberry at it.

If you've reached that stage where you don't give a stuff about image and are not embarrassed by Mother Nature's mockery then this is the book for you!

Past Your Sell-By Date Yet? is dedicated to old age and everyone who gets there.

All sanity depends on this:
that it should be a delight
to feel heat strike the skin,
a delight to stand upright,
knowing the bones are moving
easily under the flesh.

Doris Lessing

You have to
floss blancmange.

And in the end, it's not the years in your life that count. It's the life in your years.

Abraham Lincoln

PAST YOUR SELL-BY DATE YET?

Breakfast is now breakslow.

Age appears best in four things: old wood to burn, old wine to drink, old friends to trust, and old authors to read.

Sir Francis Bacon

You have to moisturise
to slip out of bed.

Age is a high price to
pay for maturity.

Tom Stoppard

'Craps' is no longer a gambling
game but a meaningful
relationship with the bog...

Age. That period of life in
which we compound for the
vices that remain by reviling
those we have no longer
the vigour to commit.

Ambrose Bierce

Sperm is now known as
'love dust'.

Age is whatever you think
it is. You are as old as
you think you are.

Muhammad Ali

Dribbling isn't just
about football...

The art of living is more like that of wrestling than of dancing; the main thing is to stand firm and be ready for an unseen attack.

Marcus Aurelius

PAST YOUR SELL-BY DATE YET?

The food on your plate
is less than your daily dose
of pills and medicine...

By the time you're
eighty years old
you've learned everything.
You only have to
remember it.

George Burns

You have to check out the
pan for the vital organs after
you've visited the toilet.

Bashfulness is an ornament to youth, but a reproach to old age.

Aristotle

PAST YOUR SELL-BY DATE YET?

'Ménage à trois' now means
eating for three.

Can anybody remember when
the times were not hard
and money not scarce?

Ralph Waldo Emerson

PAST YOUR SELL-BY DATE YET?

A 'pile up' now refers to careful
handling of haemorrhoids.

Common sense is the
collection of prejudices
acquired by age eighteen.

Albert Einstein

Finding out that
'muffin the mule' is not a
puppet show but a sexual act...

A diplomat is a man who always remembers a woman's birthday but never remembers her age.

Robert Frost

Don't be afraid of death so much as an inadequate life.

Bertolt Brecht

A bed and a bath now
come together...

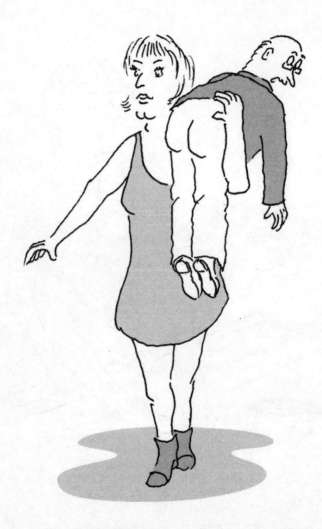

That lift from a 'tranny' isn't
quite what you expected...

'A blue tit' means you've been
too close to the freezer.

Experience is simply the name we give our mistakes.

Oscar Wilde

A wet dream is
now about toilets.

The greatest lesson in life
is to know that even fools
are right sometimes.

Winston Churchill

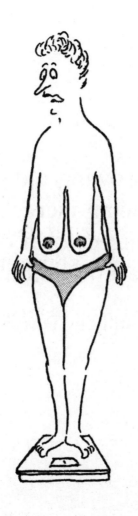

However much you diet, your tits
have a mind of their own...

Growing old is
like being increasingly
penalized for a crime
you haven't committed.

Anthony Powell

PAST YOUR SELL-BY DATE YET?

Happiness is nothing
more than good health
and a bad memory.

Albert Schweitzer

That hourglass figure now
tells the wrong time...

Putting up a tent is the nearest
you get to an erection...

PAST YOUR SELL-BY DATE YET?

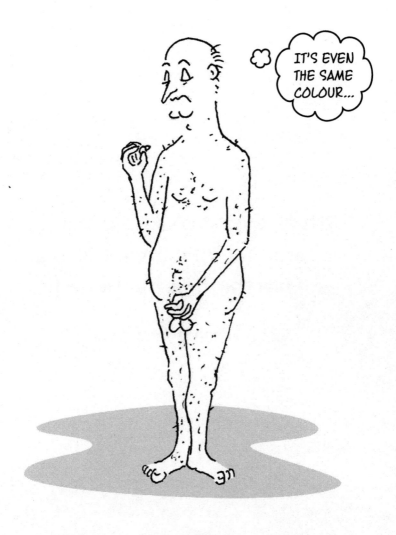

An acorn was the fruit of an oak tree
- not a comparison to your dick...

Inside every older person is a younger one... wondering what the hell happened.

Cora Harvey Armstrong

PAST YOUR SELL-BY DATE YET?

A knee trembler has nothing
to do with sex...

I see no comfort in outliving one's friends, and remaining a mere monument of the times which are past.

Thomas Jefferson

PAST YOUR SELL-BY DATE YET?

You're as old as the
woman you feel.

I don't want to get to the
end of my life and find that
I have just lived the length
of it. I want to have lived
the width of it as well.

Diane Ackerman

Being 'flash' is now when you wake
up on fire from your fag ash...

If life was fair,
Elvis would be alive
and all the
impersonators
would be dead.

Johnny Carson

PAST YOUR SELL-BY DATE YET?

It takes so long to find your now shrunken willy that you forget what to do with it when you find it...

In my youth, I stressed freedom, and in my old age I stress order.

I have made the great discovery that liberty is a product of order.

Will Durant

A 'snatch' no longer means
a fanny but a robbery.

In youth one has tears
without grief, in old age
grief without tears.

Jean Paul

PAST YOUR SELL-BY DATE YET?

Showing 'emotion' is now
handing in a stool sample.

I should have no objection to go over the same life from its beginning to the end: requesting only the advantage authors have, of correcting in a second edition the faults of the first.

Benjamin Franklin

Nature lends a hand to help
you give up smoking.

It is easy to believe that life is long and one's gifts are vast – easy at the beginning, that is. But the limits of life grow more evident; it becomes clear that great work can be done rarely, if at all.

Alfred Adler

You lose your appetite.

To keep the heart unwrinkled,
to be hopeful, kindly,
cheerful, reverent – that is
to triumph over old age.

Thomas B. Aldrich

The 'Gay Gordons'
used to be a dance...

Life is a great big canvas,
and you should throw all
the paint on it you can.

Danny Kaye

PAST YOUR SELL-BY DATE YET?

Alphabetti Spaghetti
is confusing...

You find your digestive
system is lacking.

PAST YOUR SELL-BY DATE YET?

Your pelvic floor needs
a welcome mat.

Life's tragedy is
that we get old too soon
and wise too late.

Benjamin Franklin

None of your orifices
are watertight...

Life:
a spiritual pickle
preserving the body
from decay.

Ambrose Bierce

PAST YOUR SELL-BY DATE YET?

You still hope people will
follow instructions...

Life is a sexually transmitted disease.

Guy Bellamy

A 'toss up' is more about the
start of a match than a wank...

Life is too short to
stuff a mushroom.

Shirley Conran

Vague is now exact...

Life is
one long process
of getting tired.

Samuel Butler

'Arsenic and old lace'
is no longer a novel.

Many people think old age
is a disease, something to
be thwarted if possible. But
someone has said that if any
period is a disease, it is youth.
Age is recovering from it.

T. C. Myers

Reality is out of the window...

Not only is life
a bitch but it is
always having puppies.

Adrienne Gusoff

There are occasions when
you don't want to
pinch less than an inch...

One of the worst things
that can happen in life
is to win a bet on a
horse at an early age.

Danny McGoorty

PAST YOUR SELL-BY DATE YET?

Air management
gets out of hand...

Old age is
the verdict of life.

Amelia E. Barr

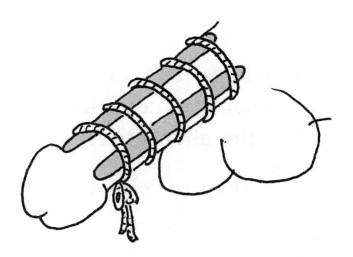

Lollypop sticks and
strings have their uses...

Old age isn't so bad
when you consider
the alternative.

Maurice Chevalier

PAST YOUR SELL-BY DATE YET?

'Give us a clue' is no longer
a game, but life...

Old age is ready to
undertake tasks that youth
shirked because they
would take too long.

W. Somerset Maugham

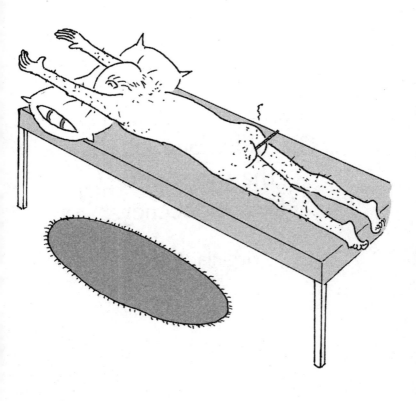

Colons are no longer
punctuation marks...

The older one grows,
the more one
likes indecency.

Virginia Woolf

PAST YOUR SELL-BY DATE YET?

Happiness is when that muscular
spasm turns out to be an erection...

Old age is far more than white hair, wrinkles, the feeling that it is too late and the game finished, that the stage belongs to the rising generations. The true evil is not the weakening of the body, but the indifference of the soul.

Andre Maurois

When a 'pain in the arse'
is only one of many...

One should never make
one's debut with a scandal.
One should reserve that
to give an interest
to one's old age.

Oscar Wilde

PAST YOUR SELL-BY DATE YET?

A woodpecker
is an artificial dick...

Old age adds to the
respect due to virtue, but
it takes nothing from the
contempt inspired by vice;
it whitens only the hair.

J. P. Senn

PAST YOUR SELL-BY DATE YET?

You feel you have to join
in any sports available...

Old age, believe me,
is a good and pleasant
thing. It is true you are
gently shouldered off the
stage, but then you are
given such a comfortable
front stall as spectator.

Jane Harrison

'Fucking' is now reserved for
the Old Age pension.

Old age
is an insult.
It's like being
smacked.

Lawrence Durrell

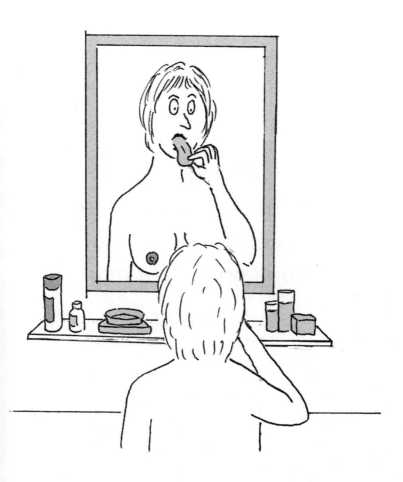

The nearest you get to a fur
coat is on your tongue...

Old age is
the most unexpected
of all the things that
can happen to a man.

Leon Trotsky

The nearest you get to grips with
a knob is opening the door.

The older I grow,
the more I distrust the
familiar doctrine that
age brings wisdom.

H. L. Mencken

'Passing wind' is not the name
of an Indian squaw...

People creep into childhood, bound into youth, sober in adulthood, and soften into old age.

Henry Giles

PAST YOUR SELL-BY DATE YET?

Anal purification is now
an exciting event.

Perhaps one has to be very old before one learns to be amused rather than shocked.

Pearl S. Buck

PAST YOUR SELL-BY DATE YET?

Thongs should only be
sold under licence.

Preparation for old age should begin not later than one's teens. A life which is empty of purpose until 65 will not suddenly become filled on retirement.

Arthur E. Morgan

PAST YOUR SELL-BY DATE YET?

The real menace in dealing with a five-year-old is that in no time at all you begin to sound like a five-year-old.

Jean Kerr

Santa Claus is now a 'toy boy'.

You have to be careful
about being too abrasive
with your washing habits...

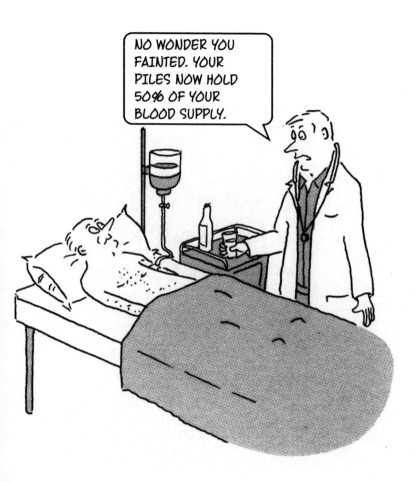

Haemorrhoids are more
than a pain in the bum...

The best thing about
the future is that it
comes only one day
at a time.

Abraham Lincoln

You experience those senior
moments more often...

The secret to staying young is to live honestly, eat slowly, and lie about your age.

Lucille Ball

'Moonies'
used to be a religious cult.

Thirty-five is a very attractive age.
London society is full of women of the highest birth who have, of their own free choice, remained thirty-five for years.

Oscar Wilde

What you thought was a road map
turned out to be varicose veins...

Threescore years and ten
is enough; if a man can't
suffer all the misery
he wants in that time,
he must be numb.

Josh Billings

Go-go dancers are
now no-no dancers.

The tragedy of old age
is not that one is old,
but that one is young.

Oscar Wilde

'Heavy metal' was lead.

The tendency of old age to the body, say the physiologists, is to form bone. It is as rare as it is pleasant to meet with an old man whose opinions are not ossified.

J. F. Boyse

Reggae was a bloke's name.

The trouble with life is that there are so many beautiful women and so little time.

John Barrymore

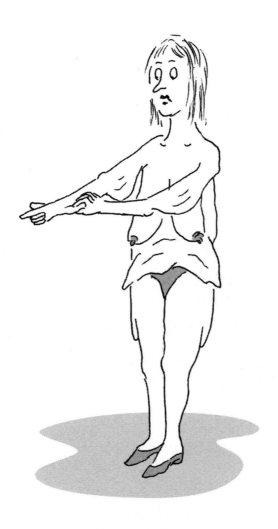

That 'with age'
weight loss has a few drawbacks.

To me, old age
is always ten years
older than I am.

Andre B. Buruch

PAST YOUR SELL-BY DATE YET?

'Bottoms up' is now an
injection not a toast...

I venerate old age; and I love not the man who can look without emotion upon the sunset of life, when the dusk of evening begins to gather over the watery eye, and the shadows of twilight grow broader and deeper upon the understanding.

Henry Wadsworth Longfellow

Simple things bring back
fond memories...

The value of old age depends upon the person who reaches it. To some men of early performance it is useless. To others, who are late to develop, it just enables them to finish the job.

Thomas Hardy

'Going potty'
has a double meaning...

When our memories
outweigh our dreams,
we have grown old.

Bill Clinton

PAST YOUR SELL-BY DATE YET?

SO, MR JONES, YOU THOUGHT 'COLONIC IRRIGATION' WAS A WATER SYSTEM IN A GERMAN CITY?

When your friends begin
to flatter you on how
young you look, it's a sure
sign you're getting old.

Mark Twain

A bowel movement is reason
to throw a party...

We do not stop
playing because
we grow old;
we grow old because
we stop playing!

Benjamin Franklin

PAST YOUR SELL-BY DATE YET?

You used to be indecisive -
now you're not so sure...

We come into this world
headfirst and go out feet
first; in between, it is all
a matter of balance.

Paul Boese

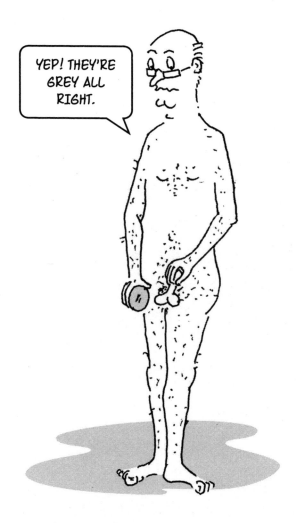

Everything in life is grey
including your bollocks...

We get into the habit of living before acquiring the habit of thinking. In that race which daily hastens us towards death, the body maintains its irreparable lead.

Albert Camus

You should
never fall asleep
in front of dogs...

We are always the
same age inside.

Gertrude Stein

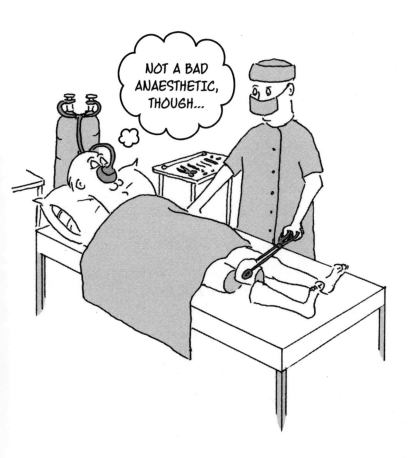

Having a joint isn't about
smoking weed any more.

Youth has
no age.

Pablo Picasso

'Casting off' was about setting out for a boating trip with a handsome young man - now it's about knitting...

Education is the best
provision for old age.

Aristotle

A CURE FOR DEAFNESS

I hope I never get so
old I get religious.

Ingmar Bergman

PAST YOUR SELL-BY DATE YET?

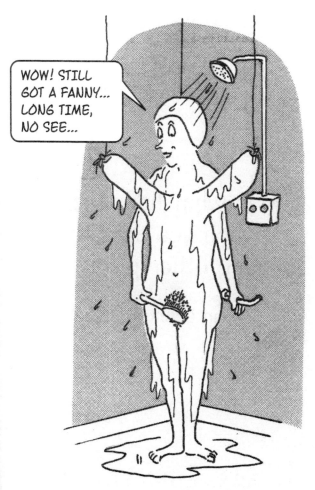

Necessity is the mother of invention, especially for those with the more ample form...

Life is what happens
when you are
making other plans.

John Lennon

PAST YOUR SELL-BY DATE YET?

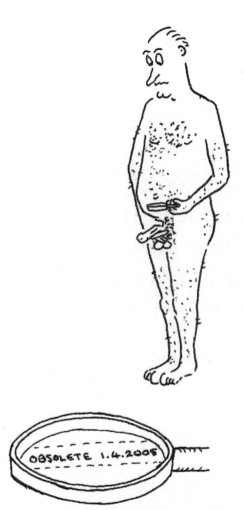

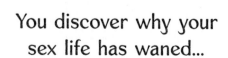

You discover why your
sex life has waned...

Remember,
a dead fish can
float downstream,
but it takes a live one
to swim upstream.

W. C. Fields

Anything for the quick life, as the man said when he took the situation at the lighthouse.

Charles Dickens

Certain parts of the body
are on the way out...

PAST YOUR SELL-BY DATE YET?

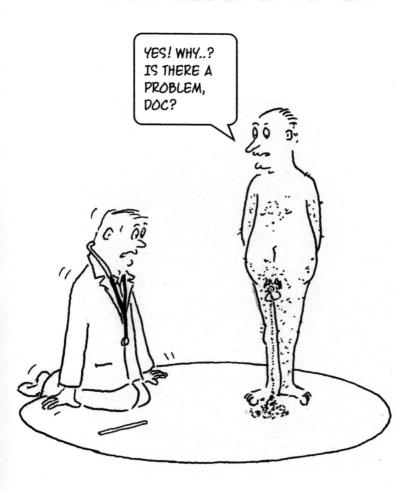

GETTING
OLD
IS WHEN...

That's it, Mr Smith. You get some rest now...

A LIGHT-HEARTED
LOOK AT THE
AGING PROCESS

Illustrations by Bob Gibbs

ISBN 1-905102-39-9
£4.99

ISBN 1-905102-81-X
£4.99

ISBN 1-905102-82-8
£4.99

All Crombie Jardine books are
available from your
High Street bookshops, Amazon,
Littlehampton Book Services, or Bookpost
(P.O.Box 29, Douglas, Isle of Man, IM99 1BQ.
tel: 01624 677 237, email: bookshop@
enterprise.net. Free postage and
packing within the UK).

www.crombiejardine.com